NOT FOR GLORY

NOT FOR GLORY

By

Margaret Burns Miles

ARTHUR H. STOCKWELL LTD
Torrs Park, Ilfracombe, Devon, EX34 8BA
Established 1898
www.ahstockwell.co.uk

British Library Cataloguing-in-Publication Data.
A catalogue record for this book is available
from the British Library.

ISBN 978-0-7223-4192-6
Printed in Great Britain by
Arthur H. Stockwell Ltd
Torrs Park Ilfracombe
Devon EX34 8BA

ABOUT THE AUTHOR

I was born in Greenock on 25 October 1952, to Robert and Helen Steele (nee Burns).

My husband George and I were married in Greenock 1 July 1970 and then moved to my mother's hometown of Aberdeen in 1974 with our two-year-old son Jason and six-week-old daughter Michelle, where we in later years adopted Tracey.

I have always enjoyed storytelling, writing and painting but have never had the opportunity to make my work known.

Now nearing sixty I intend to enjoy my 'old age', if God spares me, in doing what I love most in this beloved country that I'm blessed to live in.

I have called my first book Not for Glory as I feel very strongly about my country and the freedom that as a nation we have the right to enjoy and it was indeed for freedom that many events took place and not for glory nor riches.

May God bless my Bonny Scotland for now and ever more.

Margaret Burns Miles

ACKNOWLEDGMENTS

A very big special thanks to all my family for all their help and support and a special thank you to my two grandsons Travis Houghton and Jamie Donald, the two wee Scottish laddies and also to my great-niece Eden Steele, the wee Scottish lassie. Thanks to my brother Robert Steele for his patience and assistance preparing the work for my book.

Book cover artwork by Jason Miles at Scotland's Bothy www.scotlandsbothy.co.uk

CONTENTS

A SCOTTISH WARRIOR

I'll fight for this land with my sword in my hand
And lead all my men through each hill and glen.
From dawn until dusk we'll do what we must;
Through woodland and valley, I'll fight with my army.

We've slept in the heather and bathed in the stream
And prayed to our God to grant us our dream.
For valour and honour we'll pay with our lives
And secure Scotland's freedom for our bairns and our wives.

We'll scatter the foe, where'er they may go,
No matter how high, no matter how low.
Each nook and cranny, we'll scour them all out;
We'll see them all flee; they'll be too feart to shout.

For this land is ours, each stone and each tree,
And my men will fight to keep Scotland free,
For each living thing that grows on our land,
For each ear of corn raised by our hand.

For the love of our country and our pride in this land,
Brothers of Scotland, together we stand,
For I'm William Wallace and I vow to thee
This Bonnie Scotland I'll die to keep free.

MY LAND, MY HAME

For my land and my hame
I'll fight for my ane;
For my fields and my beasts
My sword will not cease.

No innocent blood will my sword ever see,
But only the foe who refuses to flee;
For my pride and my honour run deep in my veins
And I only fight for my wife and my wains.

So, resting a while, I'll take time to pray
And give thanks to God for blessing my day.
For my Bonnie Scotland I'll ever protect;
My duty, my brother, I'll never neglect.

I'll defend with my heart, my sword and my shield
Till my children are free to run in the fields,
So my crops can all grow without fear of a foe
And my people are safe where'er they may go.

NO SURRENDER

With no intent to slaughter or killing on our mind
We went about our business as they came up behind.
They rode upon their horses with arrows flying high.
What made them think that we would just lay down and die?

We ran towards the heather and scattered up the hill
Till we heard the Wallace shout, "Stand and fight at will."
They were not accustomed to our gullies and our glens,
Or fighting Scottish bravehearts – warriors of men.

Our Saltire's flying high as we shout the battle cry –
This flag we'll not surrender for we would rather die,
For we are Scotland's army and we know how to fight.
We'll stand beside each other late into the night.

We've guarded Scotland's Borders and sent them running home.
This country is our haven where we are free to roam.
We will not lose our heritage, our castles or our lands –
They know now what they're up against, fighting Scottish clans.

FOR LOVE OF MY COUNTRY

Heavy-hearted, sword in hand –
The fight has started to save our land.
We'll never give up; we'd rather die.
The flag that we carry is blue as the sky.

The white of the Saltire stands for what's right –
We'll carry it high right through the night.
Each Scottish warrior his home will defend,
And fight for his freedom, right to the end.

The night is now over, the fight has been won,
Our hearts are now lighter, the fighting is done;
So back to our homes as free men we go
To till our own lands, to reap and to sow.

For this Scottish soil is dear to our hearts
And will not be mastered by no foreign parts.
We'll guard it with honour, with pride and with love,
And for each day of freedom thank God above.

IN DEFIANCE

They came in their thousands to take our land;
We stood in our hundreds to make our stand.
Longshanks was eager to be our king;
The English Army would never win.

Revenge was in our minds that day,
For William Wallace we would slay.
The Bruce knew then what must be done
And vowed to fight for Scotland's sons.

Behind the Bruce our nobles fought –
The clansmen gave them all they'd got.
For every three we stood as one;
We made the English turn and run.

This land is ours, it is our home
Where we are free to run and roam.
We'll guard it well with sword in hand –
Each hill and glen, each grain of sand.

And now we fight behind the Bruce;
With England there will be no truce,
For Scottish soil will always be
The one and only home for me.

SECRETS OF THE EARTH

If the hills could tell a story of a battle fought of old,
And the stones of ruined castles let their secrets all be told,
You would hear the mighty warrior crying freedom as he fought
Defending Scotland's honour with everything he's got.

If the trees could whisper gently of the dying of a man,
And the river running boldly could reveal the warrior's plan,
You would know his only wishes were to conquer all the foe,
Securing Scotland's freedom so we could come and go.

If the tallest rugged mountains could reveal the path he took,
And the bonnie purple heather would let us have a look,
You would know how far he wandered the weather-beaten track
And see his bed of slumber he used when coming back.

If the earth revealed a secret and the Highland soil would part,
You'd see his scattered bones and his rampant Scottish heart.
And if the heavens opened and you were blessed, you'd see
The man called William Wallace who died for you and me.

BONNIE SCOTLAND

The hills are so bonnie – they sparkle with dew.
This land has been cherished for me and for you.
Through all of the ages it's always been here –
The fields and the beasts, the roaming red deer,

Bramble and briar, wood for our fire,
A bothy at night that we may retire,
The streams and the gullies with burns that run free
Give fresh running water for you and for me,

Forest and woodlands, bracken and heather,
Even the cold, wet Scottish weather,
The mountains so rugged with snow on their tops,
The farms and the meadows yielding their crops.

Beautiful Scotland, this land of my own,
Be thou for ever my beloved home,
And when the time comes that I'm ready to die
Dear God lay me down in Scotland to lie.

FAIRY FOLK OF SCOTLAND

In the night if you go walking,
You might hear the fairies talking,
Planning how to guard the glens
To keep them free from wicked men.
Scotland is the wee folk's homes –
All the elves and all the gnomes.
The Fairy Queen has hair of gold
And diamond slippers, I've been told.
In days of old they used to fly
Over the hills and high as the sky,
A watchful eye along our borders,
Carrying out the chieftain's orders.
One night a sleeping clansman lay,
An enemy not so far away .
The fairy blew into his ear
To warn him that the foe was near.
Another sang from dark till light
To help the men to rest that night,
Singing ballads of their home
So they would fight to keep their own.
The fairies spun a web of gold
Around the stronghold, I've been told,
And sprinkled diamonds in the night
To give our clansmen extra light.
They took some blue from heaven's sky
And caught a moonbeam from on high.
With love they wove them all together –
Our Saltire now will fly for ever.
So keep the fairies in your heart
And hope from Scotland they'll not part.

FOR LOVE OF SCOTLAND

Because my love for Scotland has led me on this trail
I know I fight for freedom – in this I cannot fail.
My honour and allegiance run deep within my blood –
I will not see my homeland trampled in the mud.

I'll guard these hills and glens and clear out all the foe,
Reclaiming Scottish soil wherever I may go.
My life's no longer mine to live; I gave it for my race.
These hills that lie before me will be my resting place.

My heart, my soul and spirit are Scottish to the core.
Upon my death my ghost will roam these Alba hills once more.
May the name of William Wallace be for ever in your mind,
And hold on to your freedom that I have left behind.

TWO WEE SCOTTISH LADDIES

Two wee Scottish laddies fishing by the stream –
Trying to catch a fish was their only dream.
Hiding in the woods, climbing up the trees,
Going home to mother with bruised and bloody knees,
Pretending to be soldiers riding in the glens –
Two wee Scottish bravehearts chasing all the hens.

Two big Scottish laddies starting now to grow,
To fight behind the Wallace now they want to go,
Preparing for the battle, camping by the stream –
Trying to catch the foe is their only dream.
Now they're truly soldiers riding in the glens –
Two big Scottish clansmen, warriors of men.

A GUID AULD TIME

We're singin' an' birlin' roon the room;
Abody's dancing tae the gay Gordon tune.
The pipes are blowin', the fiddler's playin' –
Fit a rare night we're a' haein'.

Hogmanay's the finest time.
Were waitin' for the bells tae chime.
The clootie dumplin's by the fire;
The coos are settled in the byre.

A' oor neebors will be soon
Almost abody in the toon,
Fur oor knees-ups are aye the best
By for we aye-wiz beat the rest.

Oor Scottish lassies ken foo tae dance;
The rest they dinna stand a chance,
An' the laddies wi' their kilts high-swingin'
Keep us goin' tae the bells start ringin'.

THE BATTLE

In the midst of our glens, we hide in our dens
While the foe they come in their tens.
They march through our lands with their sword in their hand –
No thought for woman nor man.

But deep in the valley, we know where to tarry
As we gather the clans for our army.
Through bracken and heather, we battle the weather
For we've lived in these hills for ever.
No innocent blood have we ever shed,
For we only fight to be free in our bed,

To till our own land and work with our hands,
To tend to our beasts and build up our barns.
The sun blesses the sky – our heads held high
As each man prepares to live or to die.
For this bonnie land we'll fight and we'll stand
And pray to our God we may lean on His hand.

The battle's now over; it's time to go home.
We've conquered the foe – this land is our own.
We bury the dead on this land that is ours
And carry the wounded home to their mothers.
The sun's now gone down; our campfires are bright
And we can sleep free on this blessed night.

SCOTLAND MY OWN

This Scottish soil is sacred, worth more than rich man's gold.
The tales of Bruce and Wallace for ever have been told –
They fought with truth and honour and valour to be free.
How precious is this land secured for you and me!

As I walk along the shores I see the Isle of Skye;
My heart is full of pride and I cannot help but cry –
With mountain tracks and gullies and heather in the dells,
The woodlands and the rivers and bonny rugged fells.

Oh, Scotland, how I love you! How much I cannot say;
I only know my heart would break if I should go away.
These roots of love that bind me cannot be torn apart;
For ever, Bonny Scotland, you'll stay within my heart.

HEROES IN THE PAST

I wander through the battlefield now the deed's been done –
The dying lying scattered even though we've won.
My heart is full of sorrow for the brothers that we lost;
The love they had for Scotland was gave at any cost.

The crying of the wounded lies heavy on my mind –
These men who fought and died with me, many of a kind,
Brothers, sons and fathers, lie scattered all around,
Some so badly injured, never to be found.

They're Scotland's dying heroes who gave their life this day
Defeating Edward's army, who turned and fled away.
Now as we clear the battlefield and bury all our dead
I can't believe how many for Scotland died and bled.

Forget them we shall not, for within our hearts they lie.
We'll remember them for ever when we hear the battle cry.
We're fighting with the Wallace, fighting to be free –
This land of ours is destined to belong to you and me .

A SILENT PRAYER

I hear the battle cry, and see the flag fly high.
Our swords are slaying, our hearts are praying
Let this battle be the last, may this bloody night end fast.

We have to fight to keep us free; my family all depend on me.
Their lives I hold within my hands. I pray the Lord will help me stand
That I may fight to free another – my wife and child, my friend, my brother.

The fight's now over – we have won – but I have killed another's son.
Our freedom has a price to pay, that we can live another day.
We must protect these Scottish lands; we'll not be ruled by other hands.

SEND THEM HOME

Longshanks came riding through the glen
With a bunch of his merry men.
They didna hae a soddin' clue
What the bloody Scots could do.

He said, "Oh, merry men, get ready.
Hold your horses nice and steady.
Our white and red looks quite a treat —
I think they'll bow when us they meet."

Now they were feeling very prim,
Even thinking they would win,
For when they saw the state of us
It gave them all just quite a buzz.

For we were not dressed two the same —
Oor hair as wild as horse's mane,
Wi' faces painted blue and white
We gied them a' a right good fright.

With weapons rough and all handmade
Some even hid tae use a spade,
But Scotsmen are a feisty lot —
They gave them everything they'd got.

The Wallace got his men in line
And told them, "Here and now's the time,
For Scotland's sons would now be free —
I'ts time to stand and fight with me."

Now, long years passed, the war has ended;
From those bravehearts we are descended.
We will not live no other way —
We're proud and Scots and here to stay.

THE CROFT

The croft they loved and lived in made them all feel safe –
Children running, playing, a happy family place.
Their mother peels the tatties and makes a pan of stew,
And father hunts within the woods to catch a fowl or two.
The older brothers working trying to till the land,
To earn an honest living, earned by their own hand.

Why did they have to come and burn their cottage down?
What could have been their reason to turn their lives around?
Young William had been hunting – some deer he went to track –
The murder of his family he found when coming back.
His heart was full of sorrow; his eyes could not conceive.
His family taken from him, he just could not believe.

His uncle taught him wisely; he turned into a man.
With victory and honour, he led the Wallace clan.
His life was not for living; it was destined for a cause –
He fought against the English, who came to break our laws.
We're keeping up the legacy he won for you and me;
As sons of William Wallace we're fighting to be free.

THE FLAG BOY

I'm not a full-grown Scotsman; I'm only just a boy,
But I will carry out my task with honour, pride and joy.
I've marched through many battles and lived to tell the tale,
And travelled over meadows and rugged mountain trail.

In battle you will find me leading all the rest,
Protected by my brothers, who always fight their best.
No matter what the outcome I am prepared to die,
Holding Scotland's Saltire high up in the sky.

When I'm a few years older and fighting like a man,
I'll march beside my brothers and help to hold this land.
And when the battle's over, proud that we have won,
I'll have been the Scotsman protecting someone's son.

SONS OF WALLACE

We're sons of William Wallace, and fighting to be free,
Remembering all the battles he fought for you and me.
In 1305 they killed him and tried to hold him down,
For he would not surrender to a noble English crown.

The Bruce took up the challenge that Wallace left behind;
He led the Scottish clansmen, the bravest of a kind.
The land was drenched in blood that day they fought at Bannockburn;
They gave a cry of freedom as the foe began to run.

The field is calm and peaceful now, bathed within the sun,
And gently standing with a tear a soldier beats a drum.
A piper standing by him plays a last lament
While the dead are proudly honoured, and to their graves are sent.

WAITING FOR DADDY

My daddy left this morning, for Scotland he will fight
Ah heard ma mammy greetin', long into the night.
Before ma daddy left he said, "Son, ye're near a man,
And you must help yer mammy, any way you can."

I'll get up in the morning, and muck out a' the byre,
And then I'll chop the logs, for burning in the fire.
And when I'm in my bed at night, she'll naw hear me cry.
My daddy said I must be brave, so I will have to try.

I know my daddy will come hame, he'll not stay away.
But he has to fight with Wallace, to keep the foe at bay.
Though sometimes it's so hard, when ma daddy isn't near.
But dreaming in my bed at night I pretend that he is here.

Oh, how I love my mammy, I'll not make her sad.
I winna take my beasties in the hoose 'n' make her mad!
I'll be such a good boy, she'll be so proud of me.
And for my daddy every night, she will pray with me.

My love he left this morning, to fight for what is right.
We heard oor wee boy crying, long intae the night.
My poor wee Scottish laddie, oh, how it breaks ma heart,
To see you so unhappy, when Daddy has to part.

We'll pray to God to keep him safe while fighting for this land.
So we are free to roam these glens, together hand in hand.
I'll make our hame a haven, a safe and happy place.
We'll think of Daddy always, with a smile upon oor face.

Only in ma bed I'll cry, so you won't see my tears.
I'll work along beside you, and help to calm your fears.
When Daddy's hame he'll be so proud, of you, his only son.
He'll soon be hame, ma bonnie lad, when the battle's won.

A BONNIE LAND

Smell the damp earth and feel the cool breeze;
Hear the birds sing as they fly through the trees;
See the blue sky and feel the hot sun
As the deer through the hills swiftly they run.

The horse and the ploughman are working the field
Getting the tatties laid out in dreels.
The farmers are working this hot summer day,
Ready to stack and build up the hay.

There's cows in the field chewing their cud;
The pigs are all happy basking in mud.
With bothies and shielings dotting the glens,
Crofts and wee steadings running with hens.

This peaceful life was gained at a cost –
We must never forget the ones who were lost.
They paid with their lives to keep Scotland free,
Securing this land for you and for me.

THE WEE SCOTTISH LASSIE

She gathered her flowers in the peace of the wood,
Not knowing of battles fought past where she stood.
They fought for her freedom – not glory or gain,
But only for peace for each wife and each wain.
They all gave their lives so she'd grow with no fear,
With never a care that the foe may be near.
Her life has been free of sorrow and pain –
May blood never spill in these woodlands again.
My wee Scottish lassie, sae bonnie and fair,
Wi' yon big brown eyes and the sun on your hair,
May you always be free to run and to roam
In these Scottish hills that we're proud to call home.

GOOD FREENS AT HOGMANAY

Come on, bairn, an' sit on ma knee.
Come on, bairn, it's time fur yer tea.
Yer da'll be hame soon an' gie's a wee tune.
The folks'll be ower an' dance roon the room.

The menfolk will bring their pipes an' a dram;
The wifies'll a' hae their wains in a pram.
We'll hae clootie dumpling, shortbread an' cheese,
An' a glass o' fruit wine, the young anes tae please.

There's food on the table, there's coal on the fire –
It's a lang time yit till we a' retire.
We'll hae a wee sing-song, the wifies will greet;
The mannies get boozy, an' stamp wi' their feet.

Were hoochin' an' hawin' till the clock strikes twelve,
Then a' the ill feelin's are put on the shelf.
Tomorrow's the New Year – we'll pray for good cheer
And hope oor good freens will aye-wiz be near.

MY HIELAN' LASS

Come on an' sing a song tae me, ma bonnie Hielan' lass,
For ah'm goin' tae fight the English tae save oor blade o' grass.
I'll go wi' Bruce's army for many a week an' day.
So come an' sing a song tae me before I go away.

Tomorrow when the sun comes up I will hae tae go.
I'll join with all the clansmen tae face up tae the foe.
The Bruce upon his horse will ride and lead us in the fight;
So come an' sing a song tae me this bonnie summer's night.

A ribbon I will bring you to tie yer bonnie hair –
The colour of the Saltire that flies up in the air –
And lying in my bed at night I'll keep you in my heart.
Those wicked sons of Longshanks will not keep us apart.

CLANSMEN TOGETHER

The Wallace he fought to keep Scotland free,
To preserve this land for you and for me.
There's none of us perfect; we're no lily-white,
But when it comes to our Scotland we'll do what is right.

Together like brothers we'll stand and we'll fight
Though we hid a swally the previous night.
The fights and the barneys between Scottish clans
Are a' put aside when it comes to our land.

For we'll be united to keep Scotland free –
This land will be cherished by you and by me.
After the battle we're all on our way –
We'll have a wee dram tae end aff the day.
But noo it's all back tae a bickerin' feud –
This cheap home brew is no very good.

ECHOES OF OLD

When the mist rolls ower the heather you can hear their voices sing,
And the dew falls on the mountain you can hear their laughter ring.

When the sun shines in the meadow you can hear the battle cry.
'Twas here in days long gone by many men would die.

When the moon shines on the valley around their campfires bright
You can hear them softly talking long into the night.

This land was once their home, where they were free to roam.
No foreign man would ever come to take it for his own.

They marched with truth and valour; right was on their side —
Securing Scotland's freedom so we can rule with pride.

IN THANKS FOR MY LAND

As I stand among the heather I smell the Highland scent
And think about my kinsfolk, whose blood was dearly spent.
Securing Scotland's future they fought and died at will;
They gave their lives for freedom upon these very hills.

As I stand among the heather I see my wife and child
Playing in the glen, running free and wild.
This land we'll guard with honour, we'll keep it as we ought –
I'll never walk away from it because I am a Scot.

As I stand among the heather I get down on my knees.
I'm thankful for my blessings – the air, the birds and trees.
Our Highland soil is sacred. It comes from God above.
He could not give me more than this Scotland that I love.

THE DAYS OF WALLACE

We waited in the woods that night;
The air was cool, the stars were bright.
We made a vow we'd never part;
I hold you now within my heart.

Oh, Murron, how I love you so!
I'll never ever let you go.
The holy man our vows he read –
Earth and leaves they were our bed.

No English lord your bed will share –
That's why we wed in secret there.
In daytime you would smile at me;
When darkness came I'd lie with thee.

They came on their horses into the village,
Their only concern to rule and to pillage.
My wife with her long bonnie hair caught their eye –
She never knew then she was destined to die.

I took up the fight on that dark lonely night,
Vowing to kill who had slain her on sight.
We gathered an' army and rode to the glens,
While the men in the hills they joined in their tens.

We held Scotland's boundaries; we kept them all out,
And chased them all back with a victory shout;
But fate had decided that I had to die
And soon with my Murron again I will lie.

Now as I lie here preparing to die
I know that my clansmen are waiting nearby.
No fear shall I show in front of my foe –
They'll hear Scotland's hero where'er they may go.

Murron, my love, I now see your face
As they start to kill me in this filthy place;
But as I look up to a bonnie blue sky
I'll give thanks to God, preparing to die.

They've broken my body and cut off my head
And scattered my limbs – to where they've not said –
But they could not break this brave Scottish heart,
Nor break my will, nor soul tear apart.

For I would not kiss the English lord's ring
Or ever accept him to be Scotland's king;
So my last cry of freedom is what they will hear,
To show WILLIAM WALLACE died with no fear.

DEATH OF A SCOTSMAN

I'm lying in the heather gazing at the sky.
My heart is full of sorrow – I know I'm going to die.
I hear the battle raging and my brothers all around –
There are many of us wounded lying on the ground.

I gave my sword with honour; my life I give with pride.
Never will a Scotsman run away and hide.
Please tell my wife and child I love them very much.
They're free to live and run their lives without an English touch.

The sun's gone down; it's darker now; the stars are fading fast.
It's gone all quiet round about – the battle's won at last.
An angel of the Lord has come to help us on our way,
For we only fought for freedom and to live another day.

And now that I'm in heaven I look down upon my land.
I see the rugged mountains and every grain of sand.
This truly is a nation built with pride and love –
A creation made in heaven, a gift from God above.

YESTERDAY'S HEROES

For those of you who will be born
Not for a while but a future morn
We give you the freedom to walk in this land,
Paid with our lives and the sword in our hands.

Remember your fathers from days long gone by,
How they went into battle knowing they'd die,
And so this to you our children to come:
Remember us when this day is done.

Give thanks to God that Scotland is free;
Please give thought a little for me.
I gave you my life, though I'm in the past,
So do all these things that I'm going to ask.

Cherish your families, hold them all dear,
Give them your love whenever they're near,
And think of your brother where'er he may be.
Be proud of you country, just like me.

Now it's for this land I lay down and die,
While my wife and my child look on and cry,
But deep in my heart I know we have won –
Scotland is free, the battle been done.
So as you look back may you always remember
The BRAVEHEARTS of old would never surrender.